A Friend to All

A Friend to All

A Jataka Tale

Illustrated by Rosalyn White

Dharma Publishing

Jataka Tales Series

Originally published under the title *Best of Friends*. Second edition 2009, revised and augmented with guidance for parents and teachers.

Printed on acid-free paper.

Printed in the United States of America by Dharma Press
35788 Hauser Bridge Road, Cazadero, California 95421

9   8   7   6   5   4   3   2   1

Library of Congress Control Number: 2009936420
ISBN 978-0-89800-513-4
www.dharmapublishing.com

Dedicated to
All the World's Children

Once upon a time in the Himalaya Mountains, there lived a woodpecker with brilliant feathers of many colors. Not only was this bird especially beautiful, he was also kind and intelligent. To all the other animals he was like a friend and a physician, watching over their health and giving them good advice. So kind was his heart that he did not want to harm any living creature and lived only on berries and sweet flowers.

One day while the woodpecker was flying through the darkest part of the woods, he came upon a lion rolling on his back on the ground. The lion's mane was dirty and tangled, and his cries of pain sounded so pitiful and sad that the woodpecker hurried to comfort him.

"O, King of Beasts! What has happened? Have you been hit by a hunter's arrow? Have you been wounded by a buffalo's horns or an elephant's tusks? How can I help?"

"O Physician of the Forest! Beautiful bird! A piece of bone is stuck in my throat! I cannot swallow it or cough it up. I am choking! Please save my life!"

The clever bird quickly thought of a way to help the lion. On the ground he found a stick and told the great beast to open his jaws as wide as he could. He placed the stick between the lion's top and bottom teeth. With the lion's mouth wide open, the bird boldly hopped inside to the very bottom of the throat. With his long sharp beak, the woodpecker gently began to jiggle at the bone fragment that was stuck there until he pulled it free. As he jumped out of the lion's mouth he kicked away the stick, and the big animal's misery was ended.

Filled with relief, the lion thanked the woodpecker again and again. He knew that without the woodpecker, he would surely have died in agony. And the bird, knowing he had eased another's pain, was as pleased as the lion. To bring happiness to others brought him joy, and he did not care at all if he was thanked or praised.

Later it happened that the woodpecker was unable to find food for many days. His belly ached with hunger as he flew from branch to branch in search of berries or sweet leaves. Suddenly the bird spied that very same lion beneath the trees, feasting on an antelope he had hunted down.

So hungry was the woodpecker that he longed for a morsel of the lion's meal. He landed on a branch nearby. Without asking for anything, he watched the lion devour his prey, hoping the lion would remember him and offer him some food.

Indeed the lion recognized the woodpecker who had once saved his life. But being rather greedy and proud, he ignored the bird's heroic rescue and forgot his former words of gratitude.

"Why should I, the mighty lion, bother with you, little bird?" he snarled. "This food is mine! Is it not enough that you are still alive after entering a lion's mouth? I can devour anything I please. Now away with you before I lose all patience and eat you in one bite!"

The woodpecker soared straight up into the sky with the freedom and power of birds. High up in the clouds, he met a sky sprite who had been watching the scene below and was troubled by what he had heard.

"O exalted and most beautiful of birds! Why do you allow this rude lion to insult you? Why do you not respond with anger and revenge? You have the power to blind him in a flash with your beak. You could swoop down and pluck the food from his very teeth!"

"Enough of such talk," replied the woodpecker. "The way of anger is not for me. I helped the lion in order to end his pain, not to gain a reward. If he chooses not to return my gesture, I will simply leave him alone. I do not need gratitude, so if he does not repay me, what is it to me? To be able to help a friend is its own reward."

"O great bird, how can you be kind to those who are mean to you? And how can you call that voracious lion your friend?"

"Kindness sees everyone as a friend, even those who do not understand its value," replied the woodpecker. "Every animal in this forest is my friend. Whether an animal is kind to me one day and unkind to me another day does not matter. I care about them all and count them all as friends. With so many friends, I have more than enough chances to bring joy to others."

"You are a true and constant friend," exclaimed the sky sprite. "Your heart never changes, and your courage never wavers, no matter how you are treated."

If your heart is gentle and true,
All beings will gladly trust in you.
If you befriend all you meet,
Your happiness will be complete.

My Page

Colored by _____

The Jataka Tales nurture in readers young and old an appreciation for values shared by all the world's great traditions. Read aloud, performed and studied for centuries, they communicate universal values such as kindness, forgiveness, compassion, humility, courage, honesty and patience. You can bring these stories alive through the suggestions on these pages. Actively engaging with the stories creates a bridge to the children in your life and opens a dialogue about what brings joy, stability and caring.

The Best of Friends: A Story About Kindness

A compassionate woodpecker risks his life to pluck out a bone lodged in the throat of a lion. Later, desperate for food, the bird wishes for a morsel of the lion's meal. When the arrogant lion rebuffs the woodpecker, a sky sprite suggests the bird get back at the lion. But the woodpecker refrains from harsh words or revenge, demonstrating that true friendship expects no reward.

Key Values
Kindness
Helpfulness
Unselfishness
True friendship

Bringing the story to life

You might engage the children by saying, "In this story a woodpecker comes upon a lion in trouble. Does he help this creature who can eat him? Do you think the woodpecker will make friends with the lion? Let's read the story to find out."

- How does the woodpecker save the lion? Why?
- Why doesn't the lion share his food?
- How does the woodpecker react?
- What does the sky sprite say?
- Would you have responded like the sky sprite or the woodpecker?

Discussion topics and questions can be modified depending on the child's age.

Teaching values through play

Follow up on the storytelling with creative activities that explore the characters and values and appeal to the five senses.

- Have the children construct and decorate character masks for the lion and woodpecker and sky sprite. Let the lion roar and feel his powerful teeth, and let the woodpecker feel his sharp and agile bill and powerful wings. What is it like to feel the difference in size and also ability to fly?
- The children can act out different parts of the story and switch roles. They can practice sharing and generosity as they play by seeing what it feels like...
  1) not to share food
  2) to share it.
  The one who plays the sky sprite can suggest different endings.
- Have the children retell the story in their own words from the point of view of the lion. Then have them remember a time when someone shared toys or helped them in some way.

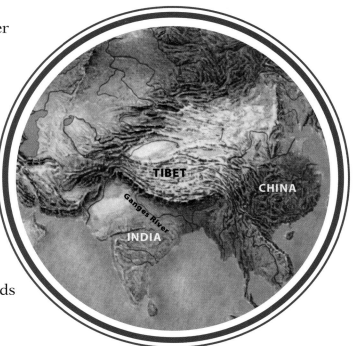

Active reading

- Before children can read, they enjoy storytelling and love growing familiar with the characters and drawings. You can just show them the pictures and tell the story in your own words with characteristic voices for each animal.
- By reading the book to them two or three times and helping them recognize words, you help them build vocabulary.
- Carry a book whenever you leave the house in case there is some extra time for reading.
- Display the key values on the refrigerator or a bulletin board – at child's eye level – and refer to them in your daily interactions.
- Integrate the wisdom of this story during challenging situations: the child might think of a time when he or she did something for someone else that wasn't appreciated. Look at the part of the story where the hungry woodpecker reacts to the lion and ask, "What would the woodpecker do? Does he get angry?" Or when things turn out unexpectedly, the children might act out the woodpecker soaring up in the sky, and feel the freedom of his wings.

Daily activities:

Talk about the story with your child while engaged in daily activities like cooking, taking care of a pet, or driving. You can point out how helpful some actions of the children have been, and also talk to them about times when they have given or received kindness. If they do have pets, you can also compare the woodpecker's caring for the lion to taking good care of the animal they love.

We are grateful for the opportunity to offer these Jataka tales to you. May they inspire fresh insight into the dynamics of human relationships and may understanding grow with each reading.

These adaptations of Jataka Tales are for children aged three to eight

JATAKA TALES SERIES

Courageous Captain
The Fish King
A Friend to All
Golden Foot
Great Gift and the Wish-Fulfilling Gem
Heart of Gold
Hunter and the Quail
Jewel of Friendship
The King Who Understood Animals
Magic of Patience
Monkey King
The Monster of Lotus Lake
Parrot and the Fig Tree
Pieces of Gold
Power of a Promise
Precious Life
The Princess Who Overcame Evil
Proud Peacock
Rabbit in the Moon
The Rabbit Who Overcame Fear
Spade Sage
Three Wise Birds
The Value of Friends
Wisdom of the Golden Goose
A Wise Ape Teaches Kindness